# Cardinal Newman
## Intercessor and Special Friend

### The Story of a Miracle

by
Peter Jennings

To Deacon Jack and Carol Sullivan
Brian, Jennifer and Jessica

*All booklets are published thanks to the generous support of the members of the Catholic Truth Society*

CATHOLIC TRUTH SOCIETY
PUBLISHERS TO THE HOLY SEE

## Contents

# Foreword

The Gospel of St John presents us with the formal prayer of Jesus to his Father. In the course of this prayer, we hear the following words: "I have given them the glory you gave to me that they may be one as we are one." (*John* 17:22) At this point Jesus is praying about us. In his prayer he asks that we share in his glory.

Now the glory of Christ is the same as the glory of the Father. It is the glory of heaven; the glory of God's majesty. Throughout the bible, there are many expressions of this glory of God. It always is a glory that stands as a corrective to human glory. Whereas we tend to the glory of our own achievements, to self-satisfaction and self-exultation, the glory of God is always different. Indeed the glory of God in Christ can be found only by way of Calvary. When Jesus is raised on the cross then his glory, and that of the Father, is truly revealed. His glory is always a gift of the Father. It is brought to its fullness in his victory over suffering and death, by the power of the Holy Spirit, and in the glory of heaven.

This booklet is a story of the glory of God. In the life of Jack Sullivan, about which we read here, there is remarkable testimony to the power of God, to God's glory.

This testimony is found, as we should expect, in the life of one man who was walking the pathway of intense suffering.

In telling the story of Jack Sullivan, this booklet also introduces us to John Henry Newman. It was in response to the invocation of Jack Sullivan to Cardinal Newman for help, for his prayers alongside those of the sick man, that this glorious miracle took place. Jack had already opened his heart to Cardinal Newman, finding in him a spiritual friend and protector. Now, in the hour of his greatest need, his friend did not let him down!

We give thanks to God for the decision of the Church that John Henry Newman will be declared Blessed. This is a great encouragement and an inspiration to people all round the world. In a very special way it is so for everyone in the City of Birmingham, in Oxford and throughout England. We are so proud that one of our own will be declared to be among the blessed. And this is true, too, for so many in the Anglican Communion, for Cardinal John Henry Newman is, in a very real sense, a person whom we share.

So many people know the name of John Henry Newman. We know him through his hymns, through the accounts of his life, with its struggles of conscience and the pain of his decisions. Many are familiar with his writings and the widespread influence of his words. His was an extraordinary intellect, dedicated to the search for truth and the service of God in the Church.

Not many people today are aware of the many years Father John Henry Newman spent as a parish priest in Birmingham. These years and this ministry are an eloquent testimony to his holiness. Indeed the declaration of this holiness is a great encouragement to all parish priests, especially in this *Year For Priests*, called for by Pope Benedict XVI.

So many people, therefore, can identity with these different aspects of the rich life of John Henry Newman. The forthcoming declaration of his sanctity encourages us all, in our prayer, in our study, in our quest for unity among Christians, in our efforts to proclaim our faith to our contemporaries. He is indeed a holy man for our age.

May John Henry Newman intercede for us as we strive to open ourselves to receive God's glory in our lives, even as Jesus promised.

Cardinal John Henry Newman, pray for us!

✠ The Most Reverend Vincent Nichols
Archbishop of Westminster
July 2009

**John Henry Newman.**

# Introduction

In this booklet we find recorded in ordinary words a most extraordinary event. We find we are witnesses to a miracle.

To the modern mind a miracle can be an uncomfortable event. We read of miracles in the pages of the New Testament, those acts performed by Jesus Christ Himself, or by His apostles. We can also read of various miracles performed by the saints of later centuries. With all of these we can say that they happened a long time ago, but now knowledge has developed, science has moved on, we can explain things differently. A miracle which happened in the 21st century is what we are considering here. People will ask: does God still work miracles in the age of computers, the internet, space travel and all the other wonders we accept so easily? The answer would seem to be "Yes". Such an answer challenges our ideas of how the world goes, and perhaps that is no bad thing.

Anyone involved in the process of promoting an individual as a candidate for canonisation by the Catholic Church knows very well that for this to happen there is the necessity of a miracle of physical healing which can be ascribed to that candidate's intercession. When Pope John Paul II altered the rules for beatification and canonisation in 1983, he legislated that one miracle is required for each stage, apart from the cases of martyrs, where just one miracle is required prior to actual canonisation. It is interesting to note in this regard that, although it would normally be the case that it is a miracle of physical healing that is presented for consideration, the regulations do make mention of "wonders of another kind", without actually specifying what these might be.

Pope John Paul canonised and beatified more men and women than any of his predecessors. Under his successor, Pope Benedict XVI, a large number have also been advanced - most noticeably several hundred martyrs from the Spanish Civil War. Apart from the martyrs, for each and every one of these new saints, a miracle of healing will have occurred through their intercession. So, rather than saying that the age of miracles is something which belongs to the Early Church or medieval times, we can assert with great confidence that we live in an age of miracles. Indeed, the miracles of modern saints have only been declared after the most painstaking medical and scientific investigations, which earlier centuries could not have imagined being possible.

Jack Sullivan's story, as it unfolds in these pages, is a part of that wonderful proof of God's love for us which every miracle speaks about. Jack's story also tells us a great deal about how the Church investigates the claims that a miracle has occurred. It is not just a matter of asserting that something miraculous has happened. It has to be proved beyond reasonable doubt that what has happened cannot be explained by modern, scientific medical knowledge. For the Church to be able to do this a great deal of evidence has to be submitted to the body responsible for investigating such claims, the Congregation for the Causes of Saints in Rome. One of the first things that must happen after a claim of a cure has been made is that the local Bishop must set up a Tribunal to investigate what has happened. The Tribunal has to interview the one who claims to have been cured and other witnesses who can vouch for what happened before and after the event. It is absolutely essential for the Tribunal to gather together all the relevant medical documents and, if possible, depositions from the doctors involved in treating the patient. This can often be difficult, given the understandable reluctance on the part of many doctors to ascribe what happened to their patients as something inexplicable or the result of divine intervention. For the Newman Cause it was extremely fortunate that the cooperation of Jack Sullivan's doctors was freely and fully given, and access to the medical records posed no insurmountable problems.

The Tribunal to investigate Jack Sullivan's case met in his home diocese of Boston, Massachusetts, under the auspices of Cardinal Sean O'Malley. The length of time required to hold the various sessions, to interview the witnesses and collate their evidence and to gather the medical documents, was rather longer than had been originally anticipated, but by November 2006 all the necessary work had been done and copies of the hundreds of pages that had been assembled were finally forwarded to Rome.

It would not be feasible for everyone involved in the Roman process to read over every one of the pages of evidence submitted in any given case. Therefore, one of the first tasks that has to happen, once the Congregation for Saints is satisfied that the Diocesan Enquiry has done its work properly, is that the Roman Postulator of the Cause has to produce a summary of the findings - in fact, the document he edits is called the *Summarium*. The Roman Postulator for Cardinal Newman's Cause is Dr Andreas Ambrosi. He is a well-known and much respected member of the College of Postulators and has helped many Causes reach a successful conclusion. Dr Ambrosi and his secretarial team worked very hard and the *Summarium* of the Sullivan case was soon published, a feat all the more remarkable because much of the original English had to be translated into Italian.

After the completion of the *Summarium* the next stage of the Roman process involves the doctors. The Congregation for the Causes of Saints has a list of medical experts whom it can call upon to evaluate and judge the cases of presumed miraculous healing that are submitted. If these doctors feel they lack expertise in any given area they are permitted to bring in another expert from outside their ranks. Initially two doctors are nominated, neither knowing who the other one is, and these are required to give a preliminary verdict on the evidence. This is helpful as an indication of what informed medical expertise has to say about the case under review, and is also crucial because at least one of the two must give a positive opinion for the case to be referred to the full Medical Council. After these initial soundings, the case is handed over to this council, the "Consulta Medica", as it is known in Italian, and from this long list of doctors, five come together to give a final verdict, which is reached by majority vote. We know that when the doctors voted on Jack Sullivan's case on 24 April 2008, they were unanimously in favour of the view that what had happened to him was inexplicable in terms of medical knowledge.

Obviously a lot depends on this vote of the Medical Council. If it is not successful - as sometimes happens - the case must be rejected. If it is successful, as it was for Jack Sullivan, things move to the next level, that of the Theological Consultors. Seven theologians are appointed and these have the task of examining the case to see whether the inexplicable medical event was indeed miraculous. They must needs examine who was invoked, by whom, for how long, and with what end in view. Their verdict will indicate that there was a direct link between the invocation of the Servant of God and the resulting miraculous cure.

After this important milestone was passed, on 23rd April 2009, the matter was referred to the Ordinary Session of the Congregation as it is known, when the Cardinals and Bishops, who form the highest level of any Vatican department, met and voted on the cure. This took place on 2nd June 2009, and, as it was unanimously in favour, the whole case was sent to Pope Benedict XVI for his approbation and the issuing of the Decree announcing the miracle and formally accepting it as of God. Moving rather quickly, the Papal Decree was promulgated on 3rd July 2009, only a month after the decision of the Cardinals. The Decree also opens the way for the fixing of a date and place for the Beatification or Canonisation ceremony.

Very early on in his Pontificate, Pope Benedict XVI reverted to earlier custom and announced that in future while Canonisations would normally be done in Rome, as acts of the Universal Church, it was better to do Beatifications locally, in the Diocese where the candidate lived. This change is designed to involve the local church more and to encourage the faithful in devotion to the particular saints of their area. Even though the Beatification ceremony will be in the city where Cardinal Newman lived for so many years, his significance is much more widely felt than in Birmingham alone. The interest in his Cause has been worldwide, as shown by the growing calls for him to be made a Doctor of the Church, which have come from all quarters of the globe.

The Beatification of John Henry Cardinal Newman, as a result of the miracle described in these pages, is an event which many in the Church have longed for and worked towards for a considerable period of time. The great Popes of the twentieth century praised his life and writings. Pius XII, Paul VI and John Paul II all wrote and spoke about their hopes that one day Cardinal Newman would be raised to the honours of the altar and be a light and a guide for the whole church in difficult times. It is under Pope Benedict XVI, who has also studied and admired the "great English Cardinal", that the event is finally taking place.

When John Paul II declared Newman "Venerable" in January 1991, thereby recognising his eminent holiness of life, many thought that the Beatification would follow on very quickly. It was not to be. It is not possible to produce a miracle to order, as I hope I have shown, and although various earlier cases were examined - all of them interesting and moving in their own right - none ultimately stood up to the intense scrutiny the Church requires. Patience and prayer proved necessary, until Jack Sullivan, almost accidentally, discovered Cardinal Newman and turned to him in the great crisis of his life.

What is described in this fascinating pamphlet, much of it in Jack Sullivan's own words, is not the end of the story as far as the Cause of John Henry Newman is concerned. It is marvellous to have reached the moment of the Beatification, but those who love the Cardinal will not rest until he is a canonised saint of the Church. So the work will go on and many prayers will be said to achieve that end and to realising another miraculous cure through his intercession. When that will happen we do not know; where it will happen we cannot say; that it will happen is the fervent prayer of so many, and I hope it will be the prayer of all who read this booklet and are inspired by what they find in its pages.

*Fr Paul Chavasse, Provost,*
*The Oratory, Birmingham, July 2009*

# Miracle Healing

## The Feast of the Assumption, Tuesday 15th August 2001

This is Jack's story in his own words: "This morning the pain was just as intense as the day before; it was so horrifying that I was put on morphine. It would come in waves, with intervals about 20 seconds apart during which I had to adjust my position slightly. Earlier than I anticipated the same therapist came in and announced that it was time for my walk. I was surprised that she had arrived so early and wanted me to walk with the aid of a walker. I was upset because I hadn't been given any medication to help control the pain. I asked her to come back and see me later but she told me that it was now or never, meaning it would not happen until she came back the following day.

"I found it excruciatingly painful just to move onto the right side of my bed. Even with her help it took me more than five minutes. At times I had to stop and catch my breath the pain was so severe; with her help I finally twisted myself over the bed with my legs touching the cold floor. I had to stop in this position with my elbows and forearms supporting me on the bed.

"My situation appeared to be hopeless because the classes for my fourth and final year of formation were

**Jack Sullivan.**

scheduled to start in three weeks' time. I silently, but fervently, prayed to Cardinal Newman for his urgent help. I will never forget the simple words that I said that morning: 'Please Cardinal Newman, help me to walk so I can return to my Diaconate classes and be ordained.'

"Suddenly, I felt a very warm sensation all over my body and a sense of real peace and joy. I began to shudder and felt a very strong tingling sensation, which gripped my entire body. It lasted for what seemed a very long time, and was very strong. Then I felt a surge of strength, confidence and a tremendous sense of peace and joy that I could finally walk, and I was completely free of the crippling pain.

"My healing became remarkably and unexplainably accelerated in one moment of time - the doctors had previously estimated that my recovery would take anything between eight months and a year. I smiled and refused the walker that I had been given. For the first time in several months I was now walking upright, normally, and felt real power and strength in both my legs.

"Having been in bed for so long I still needed the cane for support. I walked with my therapist for more than 30 yards down the corridor past the nurse's station. I then descended and ascended a flight of stairs without any difficulty pain free. I was supremely happy and my whole person was filled with a sense of love, peace, and well-being that I had never before experienced.

"The therapist was truly amazed and she turned and said: 'Jack, you have passed with flying colours this morning and can now go back to your room and I will authorise your discharge from the hospital.' I just wanted to walk and walk. I wanted to walk down to the other end of the corridor where there was a large window, plants, and chairs, much like an atrium. The therapist told me that this was not necessary. I insisted because I had not walked normally and free from pain for many months.

"I stood by the windows thrilled with the beautiful scenery. She suggested several times that I sit down in an easy chair. I replied that it wasn't necessary because I was just so thrilled to be standing upright and not bent over double. We stood there for about 15 minutes and then walked back to my room. The nurse telephoned my wife Carol and asked her to come to the hospital and take me home.

"From that moment, on the Feast of the Assumption 2001 to this day in 2008 the pain has never once returned and I continue to walk normally with no restrictions and with full mobility.

"I got dressed and Carol arrived shortly afterwards. The nurses insisted that I sit in a wheelchair to be taken to the entrance but I insisted that I could walk out of the hospital unaided. They told me that I would not be discharged unless I complied, and so I reluctantly agreed to be wheeled.

"The head nurse warned me to be extremely careful about bending, turning or twisting. She also told me that I should use a cane when getting up from my bed or a chair. I was given a bottle of painkillers and told to take two every four hours. I took two pills before bed that first night just as a precaution, for I was pain free. Since that moment I have never needed to take any further medication for the pain caused by my extremely serious spinal disorder."

# An Ordinary Life

## Early life

Jack Sullivan was born on 19th October 1938, in Everett, near Boston, Massachusetts, in the United States. He was the eldest of four children. His father, Arthur J Sullivan, was a Catholic, but his mother, Dorothy A Duncan was a Presbyterian. Jack was baptised less than a month later, on 13th November, at St Mark's Church in Dorchester, where his parents lived at the time.

Jack's mother was the daughter of Reginald and Emily (Hill) Duncan. They were of Scottish ancestry, and both had migrated from St John's, New Brunswick, Canada during the early 1900s. Reginald Duncan was in charge of the composing room of the country's oldest Catholic newspaper, *The Pilot*, serving the Archdiocese of Boston.

Jack Sullivan's great-grandfather, John Henry Sullivan, came from County Cork in Ireland, along with two close friends, John Fitzgerald, and Patrick Kennedy who was the grandfather of the future President John F Kennedy. John Sullivan, a successful banker, established the Columbia Trust Company, in East Boston. He also became a well-known politician serving in the state legislature as a state senator. He employed Joseph Kennedy, the son of his friend Patrick, in the Columbia Trust Company. This opportunity propelled Joseph in his career and he took over the bank when Jack's great-grandfather died.

With the help and encouragement of John Sullivan, Joseph Kennedy became involved in politics and this led eventually to his appointment as Ambassador to the Court of St James in London. John Sullivan helped to bring together Joseph Kennedy and Rose, his future wife.

The friendships between the Sullivans, Kennedys and Fitzgeralds were recorded by Jack's great-aunt, Helen O'Neil, who served as the highest-ranking woman in the US Army in the Second World War.

## Jack's parents

Jack remembers his father as "a rough and tumble", self-made man. "Dad was severe with his children, especially with me, but he always had in the back of his mind the idea of instilling values such as honesty and integrity. While projecting a disciplined and tough exterior, he was an emotional and self-giving person. He was an honest, hard-working and successful businessman with a defined set of values and sense of follow-through. If he said he would do something, he always kept his word."

Jack's father worked full-time and financed his own college education as a mechanical engineer, going to classes at night. He tried to enter the military at the beginning of the Second World War but was told he was needed as an engineer and chief estimator at the Boston naval shipyard. He would work out the damage caused to a ship and the materials needed to repair it before it reached port. The shipyard was located in South Boston and Chelsea, and some of Jack's first memories were of an apartment overlooking the shore.

After the Second World War the Sullivan family moved to Braintree, Massachusetts, about 15 miles south of Boston. It was there that Jack's father, an astute businessman, started a new firm, AJS Piping Co Inc - involved in the fabrication and erection of heavy duty piping used in factories and power plants, oil refineries and chemical plants. At home, Jack's father could be bad-tempered and severe.

His mother, on the other hand, was a housewife with a heart of gold. She lived for her husband and children. Jack remembers his mother with great affection. "She was quiet and unassuming. She instilled in all of us a sense of dignity and respect for life. She had a heart of gold and always spoke up for the underdog. She was a humble and compassionate person."

## Family life

Jack has one sister, Beverly, and two brothers, Bill and Dick. All of the Sullivan children suffered from the learning disability dyslexia, and this caused difficulties in their schooling.

Beverly married a well-known professional football star, Bob Dee, who played for the Boston Patriots. His name was placed in the American Football League's 'Hall of Fame', and his number "89" was retired.

Jack was not brought up in an idyllic Catholic home. His parents were not churchgoers: "Going to church and praying did not become a prominent part of my life until I went to college at the age of 18. My parents had an unfortunate experience with the Catholic Church when they were married. Because my mother was a Protestant, the local Catholic priest forbad them to be married in church. The best he could do was to allow them the use of the living room in the rectory, with only enough room for the parents and best man and maid of honour. My mother and father were deeply hurt and basically wrote off religion as a result of this negative experience.

"As a result, I only occasionally attended St Francis of Assisi Catholic Church in South Braintree, the town where I grew up. Like my two younger brothers and my sister, I was frightened by the austerity of the local Catholic Church and its Parish Priest."

At his Confirmation Jack took the name Michael, after St Michael the Archangel. He also began to read the lives of the great saints, in particular St Teresa of Avila and St John of the Cross. He was deeply impressed with all the obstacles they encountered and overcame in total reliance on God's merciful providence: "These great saints were especially meaningful to me because during the period of my young adult life and as a child I had suffered from a number of health issues. I was plagued with a serious skin condition from infancy, which seemed to get worse as I got older and more active. The condition was a form of eczema that formed an unsightly redness and cracking of skin on my hands, arms and my legs. I was also afflicted with respiratory allergies. As a result I was always conscious of the unsightly appearance of my hands, but still managed to play sports such as baseball and football in High School."

**Learning difficulties**

Jack being the oldest child, his father was severe with him. He was successful in business and Jack found it hard to measure up to his father's expectations. Jack suffered from a learning disability called dyslexia that made it very difficult for him to read and write. As a result of these learning difficulties, Jack found it hard to relate to other people, especially at High School: "Suffering from low self-esteem, shy and a loner, I would often go fishing by myself at a nearby lake and stay and fish all day. I learned to love and appreciate nature and how all of God's creatures were so inter-dependent. Later, I became impressed with all St Teresa endured while yet maintaining a sense of humour and remaining steadfast in her faith. Since my wonderful healing on 15th August, the Feast of the Assumption, 2001, I pray daily and converse with my great special friend, Cardinal John Henry Newman."

Jack attended Braintree High School from 1953 to 1957, studying from Grade 1 through to Grade 12. He did not do particularly well and had difficulties, particularly with literature, due to his dyslexia. One member of staff told Jack that he should not plan to attend college or even apply. "You're not college material," he was told emphatically. However, this only made Jack determined to prove himself.

Prayer was not a part of Jack's life as a young man, though he had a keen sense of the conflict between good and evil. A pivotal moment occurred in Jack's life and in his spiritual development when his mother was received into the Catholic Church in 1953. Jack began to attend Mass regularly and prayer found a significant place in his life. He also began to read the Holy Scriptures: "At the time I was deeply moved by the realisation that the all-powerful Son of God was so kind and merciful to others, especially the sick, the insignificant, and the lonely - very different from the world I experienced. Jesus was kind and merciful, even to sinners and the under-privileged and I suppose I cast myself in this category. I felt a great deal of comfort and consolation as well as spiritual energy when reading about our compassionate Lord."

One of Jack's favourite parts of the Bible was the account of Jesus curing the ten lepers: "I could identify with them as I had so often been shunned in the past because of my skin condition. The point of this healing is that Jesus showed transparency in terms of His Father's love for us all. He didn't heal the lepers on the spot, but told them first to show themselves to a priest to certify their healing. He didn't take the credit. Also, out of the ten who were cured only one returned to thank him. I like to think, while reflecting on the totality of my life, that I would be like that one. I have also been drawn to the story in Luke about the prodigal son who learned to rely on his Father's love through the experiences of his life and misfortune."

It was at this time that Jack began to develop a devotion to Our Lady, reflecting upon how she, like her Son, sacrificed herself for others. Like many young people, Jack was uncertain about the direction of his life after High School. He was unsure about joining his father's firm because he had little mechanical ability.

## Vocation

For a brief period in his life, Jack felt that he was called to the Priesthood. This happened while he was a student at Stonehill College, run by the Holy Cross Fathers: "I was 20 years old at the time and I remember the event as if it was yesterday. I was praying and I suddenly felt a tremendous sense of peace and well-being; it was very strong and lasted for more than five minutes. I had utterly no control over myself, or what was happening to me. I also felt an intense presence of God and was certain He initiated this experience. I had never felt so much joy or peace before.

"I began to understand the importance of my Catholic Faith. I had received the gift of faith by the Holy Spirit. This experience completely changed my outlook and the course of my life. I had been going only occasionally to Mass, and I hadn't been to the Sacrament of Reconciliation and Penance since my Confirmation. Now, I had a strong desire to see one of the priests for a general confession."

Arrangements were made for Jack to enter Holy Cross Seminary, the following year. The effect of this experience at Stonehill College dramatically changed Jack's life as well as his thinking.

### Law career

Despite his desire to serve the Lord, in time he perceived that for him this was not to be through the Priesthood. In 1961, he left the seminary, uncertain exactly what career he should pursue. After some consideration he thought that the idea of working in the Foreign Service for the State Department might be interesting. He applied to and was accepted by Georgetown University School of Foreign Service for their Masters Degree Programme in Washington, DC.

However, after two years, in August 1963, Jack decided to return to Boston and apply to Suffolk Law

School. He was accepted and after three years graduated with the "jurisdoctor" degree and then shortly afterwards passed the bar exam for entry into the practice of law. In November 1969 he was admitted to the bar in Boston State Supreme Judicial Court Chambers.

After thirteen years of private practice Jack applied for the position at Plymouth District Court. He was selected as the First Assistant Magistrate and sworn in on 11th November 1980. Although Jack worked hard this was a particularly difficult period in his life, due to various administrative and personality difficulties in the District Court. This situation lasted for ten years and Jack bore it with great fortitude and faith.

In January 1991 circumstances changed and Jack was appointed Chief Magistrate at Plymouth District Court, a position he still holds. The original Court House, built in 1820 when James Monroe was President, is located in downtown Plymouth. The building offers views of Plymouth harbour - the very place where the Pilgrim Fathers, who in December 1620 had sailed from Plymouth, (England) in the Mayflower, had landed to start the New England States. In summer 2007 the Plymouth Court House was relocated to a fine new purpose-built complex in a different part of town. Jack, then aged 69, is now looking to retire from his work at the Plymouth Court House sometime during 2010 and concentrate on his ministry as a permanent deacon, which, as we shall see, he has now become.

## Marriage and children

In 1968 Jack began a friendship with Carol Mulvee, the girl who was to become his wife. Carol came from a stalwart Catholic family. Her uncle, Fr Robert Mulvee, was ordained priest in the diocese of New Hampshire, and later became Bishop of Providence in Rhode Island, retiring in 2005. Carol has always been a great support to Jack.

Carol and Jack were married at St Timothy's Catholic Church in Norwood, Massachusetts on 26th April 1969, in the presence of her uncle, Msgr Mulvee, who at the time was working in the Diocese of Manchester. Jack and Carol first lived in an apartment in Weymouth, Massachusetts. Carol, a high school teacher, got a job in the business department at nearby Weymouth South High School.

Carol and Jack wanted children and waited six years for a child. "At the time we were told we couldn't have children so we applied to an adoption agency associated with Catholic Charities in Boston and after a year's wait received our first child, Brian, when he was five weeks old. We were given just one day's notice! He was born on 26th February 1975 and we brought him home in late March. After Brian arrived at our home I can't adequately describe how our lives changed when one considers all of the fishing trips, baseball games and questions asked and answered."

Brian brought them great happiness and so they decided three years later to apply to Catholic Charities again and in 1978 adopted their daughter Jennifer, who was born on 26th May, the Feast of St Philip Neri, 1515-1595 (Founder of the Congregation of the Oratory, which Fr Newman joined and established in England during 1848). "She has had a featured recurring role in a critically acclaimed TV show and is the host of a travel programme."

Three years and three months later, almost to the day, Carol gave birth to their youngest child, Jessica. Jack and Carol moved to Marshfield, a town about 24 miles south of Boston, shortly after the birth of Jessica.

## The Diaconate

Jack considers his marriage as the springboard for his spiritual journey, which eventually led to ordination to the Diaconate. It was in 1995 that Jack met a deacon who suggested that he might consider service to the Church in the Diaconate. After a period of reflection and prayer, Jack spoke to his wife Carol and his Parish Priest, and others whose judgement he respected. As a result he applied in the following year for admission as a candidate for Diaconate formation in the Archdiocese of Boston.

Unfortunately an immediate difficulty arose as Jack himself explained: "As part of the admission process Carol and I met with the director, Deacon Leo Donahough and his wife. They explained that Carol would also be required to attend the first year's classes, and participate to some extent during the last three years. Therefore, she had to endorse my petition. Carol told them that although she didn't mind my involvement, she was reluctant to take on the commitment of attending classes herself, stating: 'That's his thing, not mine'."

Rather than have his application rejected, Jack asked them to put it on hold for the next class due to start in two years' time. During those two years Jack read intensely and widely. In particular he read the Bible (twice) and biblical commentaries. He studied Church history and Christology.

Jack also prayed to Our Lady that Carol might somehow change her mind. His prayer was answered the night before the application letter was due to be submitted for the next class, beginning in September 1998. Jack described it in this way: "Carol did a complete reversal. Our Lady got through."

### Serious back problems

Having overcome the initial difficulties of beginning the course for the Diaconate Jack had a shock lying in store for him. After having completed two years of his studies he developed a serious back problem. His doctors proposed surgery and told him to abandon the formation programme.

**Deacon Jack Sullivan.**

# Jack's Illness and Healing

## The First Event

### Tuesday 6th June 2000

On this particular morning Jack Sullivan woke up with serious debilitating pain in his back and both legs. He was taken to the Jordan Hospital in Plymouth, Massachusetts and the physician in the Emergency Room ordered that he be given a CAT scan. The scan revealed a serious succession of spinal disc and vertebrae deformities in the lumbar area from L2 to L5. Jack's spine was badly herniated causing severe stenosis in both legs.

The mystery was that there was no evidence of any previous trauma or history of any chronic spinal deformity to warrant this condition. The doctor explained that the vertebrae and discs were depressed inward seriously intruding upon the spinal canal, squeezing his spinal cord and femoral nerves. Jack was advised to seek treatment immediately from specialists in Boston.

Jack was concerned that it would take a long time to get an appointment to see a neurologist for a thorough examination, and before a full diagnosis of his condition could be made and any surgery performed.

Jack was gripped by tension and anxiety because he was scheduled to resume his third year of Permanent Diaconate formation classes on 5th September 2000. The third year was considered the most intensive and demanding year of the four-year formation process.

To add to these demands, immediately following classes Jack would have to undergo a four-month pastoral internship programme at a Boston hospital. While waiting for the surgeon's appointments, which seemed forever, it soon became apparent to him that surgery was essential and that the period of recuperation would almost certainly prevent him from returning to his classes.

If he consented to the surgery, as he knew deep in his heart that he must, it would almost certainly mean that he would have to drop out of the Diaconate Formation Programme. To make matters worse, Jack was now in constant and extremely severe pain. With great difficulty he managed to walk but he was completely hunched over, with his head facing the ground.

### Monday 26th June 2000

Jack was faced with a terrible dilemma: what should he do for the best? Flicking through the television channels at home one evening he came to Mother Angelica's EWTN channel. A programme about the life and teachings of Cardinal Newman caught his attention. The host, Father John McClosky, was interviewing an English priest, the distinguished Newman scholar Fr Ian Ker, who mentioned that the process for Cardinal Newman to be declared a saint required two miracles of physical healing. The first one would be required before Cardinal Newman could be beatified and declared Blessed. Towards the end of the programme the audience was asked to send details of any extraordinary experiences or healings that resulted from prayer of intercession to Cardinal Newman. The name and address of Father Paul Chavasse, Provost of the Birmingham Oratory, was put up on the screen towards the end of the programme.

"I had heard about Cardinal Newman but I did not know much about his life. I felt a very strong compulsion to pray to Cardinal Newman with all my heart. 'Please help me to somehow get back to classes so that I can be ordained and serve the Church as a Permanent Deacon,' I pleaded! I didn't pray particularly for healing but for greater persistence and courage in my life to face the challenges of each day. Immediately after my prayer, I suddenly experienced a new and uplifting sense of trust and confidence. I knew deep in my heart that something would happen as a result of my supplications to Cardinal Newman."

### Wednesday 27th June 2000

"The next morning I got out of bed virtually pain free and began to walk with little difficulty, whereas the day before I was completely hunched over. At the time I had to place my right hand on my right knee to support myself when attempting to walk one step at a time. The joy of that first moment filled my heart with gratitude to God for the intercession of Cardinal Newman."

The following day Jack had an appointment to see the chief neurologist at the Brigham & Women's Hospital in Boston. He told Jack that surgery was now unnecessary as the pain had gone and that he could return to his classes but to come back if the pain returned.

### Tuesday 18th July 2000

Jack had an appointment with Dr Gregory Brick, who was alarmed at the results of the MRI scan. Dr Brick could not understand why Jack was pain-free and could walk normally. He arranged for Jack to have a Myelogram - special dye and X-rays to make pictures of the bones and the fluid-filled space between the bones in the spine.

At a follow-up appointment, Dr Brick gave Jack the results. These showed that the vertebrae and accompanying discs were closing upon and squeezing the spinal canal, both below and above the affected area. In fact, Dr Brick pointed out significant bulges in the spinal cord above and below the affected area through which the dye couldn't penetrate. He told Jack that there was a very high risk of the complete loss of his lower functions and the probability of paralysis unless surgery was performed. A date was set for 12th September that year.

"I was mentally and emotionally overwhelmed by this prognosis. I continued to pray each day to Cardinal Newman, as it appeared that something extraordinary was happening to my body as evidenced by the absence of pain and the strength in my legs, as well as the fact that I could walk upright with ease despite the very poor physical condition of my spine."

Jack consulted with his primary care physician, Dr Lorenz Cueni, at Plymouth where he worked. Dr Cueni referred Jack to Dr Robert Banco, a Catholic, who had the reputation of being one of the best spinal surgeons in the United States. Dr Banco, chief of spinal surgery at the New England Baptist Hospital in Boston, agreed to see Jack on 5th October 2000. Prior to his appointment, Jack telephoned Dr Banco who suggested that he return to his classes and put off the surgery arranged for him at the Brigham Hospital.

## Thursday 5th October 2000

Jack had his initial consultation with Dr Banco. A thorough examination showed that he was not suffering from any pain and that he had full mobility in his back and in his legs. Dr Banco drew Jack's attention to his X-ray and told him the lack of pain was unexplainable from a medical and scientific standpoint. He told Jack that he had regained sufficient function in his back to return to his Diaconate classes.

"Dr Banco told me that he would continue to monitor my condition and that if the pain returned then I was to contact him immediately. He told me that my freedom from pain could not possibly last for long and he scheduled surgery for the second day of my Christmas vacation. This surgery did not occur. I firmly believe that my daily prayers to return to my Diaconate classes, through the intercession of Cardinal Newman, had been answered in a dramatic way."

The months went by and Jack remained free from pain and he started his busy third semester with classes from September to April and then a mandated internship programme from May through till early September 2001. Afterwards Jack had to resume classes without a break for the fourth and final year of formation.

**Sunday 22nd April 2001**

"Then, as suddenly as the pain had left me, it returned just before my last class. It was so severe that I had to leave our closing retreat celebrating the end of classes for the academic year. I explained my situation to the programme director. The pain was more excruciating and debilitating than it was the previous summer. I was now faced with the physical demands of our summer internship programme at the Brigham & Woman's Hospital in Boston. This programme was required for entry into the fourth and final year of the formation process and was scheduled to start on 15th May 2001. I prayed to Cardinal Newman that I would have the strength and stamina to complete my training for the Permanent Diaconate."

Jack concludes what he describes as "the first event" by quoting from Dr Banco's analysis in his medical records dated 3rd December 2002. Dr Banco wrote: 'I thought his symptoms (absence of pain) were resolved because the disc herniation had improved, (disc worked its way back to its normal position). However, the MRI scan 15th May 2001 demonstrated that Jack had persisting disc herniation at 13-4, which was very large, markedly compressing the L4 nerve root, creating severe stenosis and lateral stress stenosis. In fact, there was no improvement (change in the disc's position) whatsoever in his radiographic studies between his initial visit on 5th October 2000 and follow up visit on 18th May 2001. Because of this persisting and severe stenosis, I have no medical explanation for why he was pain free and for so long a time. The objective data, CT, myelogram, and MRI demonstrated that his pathology did not at all change, but his symptoms (pain) improved drastically."

## THE SECOND EVENT

The "Second Event", as Jack describes it, was even more extraordinary than the first. Although the pain in his back had returned on 22nd April 2001, his surgery was not due to take place for nearly four months, on 9th August. Jack was deeply concerned that he would not be able to return to his Diaconate classes to complete his fourth and final year. To complicate matters still further, he had to complete a 120 hours mandated internship programme by September. At the time of his surgery Jack would still have 20 to 25 hours of this programme to complete. Jack prayed, asking for Cardinal Newman's intercession that he would somehow be able to finish his internship and ultimately be ordained to the Permanent Diaconate.

**Friday 4th May 2001**

Jack telephoned Dr Banco's office and reluctantly told the secretary that the severe pain in his back and legs had returned. He asked if the date of his surgery might be brought forward. Dr Banco suggested that Jack try a less restrictive form of treatment and arranged for him to have a steroid spinal injection on Tuesday 6th June.

**Tuesday 15th May 2001**

Jack began his internship with three other classmates that evening at the Brigham & Woman's Hospital in Boston. Those first nights the pain was so bad that one of his classmates insisted that Jack sit in a wheelchair and allow himself to be wheeled around the hospital. It was not an auspicious start. The hospital was large and Jack was deeply concerned about how he would be able to manage the programme throughout the entire summer. The Chaplain and the Director of Diaconate formation were apprehensive about Jack's state of health.

"I prayed continuously to Cardinal Newman that the Lord might give me strength and courage to continue, dedicating my hospital ministry to him. I would be God's instrument, walking hunched over to help support and comfort those assigned to me from various wards and to share with them my own experiences of pain, uncertainty, and anxiety. I also remembered Dr Brick's warning that if I persisted with such physical activity, I was likely to develop severe complications. This was confirmed by another MRI scan."

## Wednesday 6th June 2001

Jack arrived at the Baptist Hospital for his steroid injection. The doctor reviewed his latest X-rays and said that Jack's condition was far too serious for him to go back to work or to continue with his classes.

Jack remembered that particular doctor telling him that in the 17 years that he had been administering spinal cortisone injections, Jack's back was the worst that he had seen. He asked the doctor to give him the injection in the hope that the treatment might help him. At the time, he was working full time at the Court and two nights a week at the hospital for five to six hours each night. Jack prayed that Cardinal Newman would somehow help him to get through each day.

**Monday 12th June 2001**

Less than a week later, Jack's pain was not subsiding and he now realised that surgery was the only answer. He telephoned Dr Banco's office. His secretary informed Jack that Dr Banco was away during all of July and was completely booked until the end of October.

**Feast of SS Peter & Paul, Friday 29th June 2001**

Dr Banco telephoned Jack and apologised for his delay in getting back to him. Jack will never forget Dr Banco's words on that occasion: "Hi Jack, sorry for the delay. How about 9th August? Is that all right with you?"

**Wednesday 8th August 2001**

By now Jack had managed to complete more than 90 hours of his internship programme. This day before his surgery he had a real sense of peace about the situation and felt that God was with him in a special way.

Later that day Jack received a clear sign that all would go well. His wife Carol, who had been very reluctant about him entering the Diaconate Programme, presented him with a beautiful hand-made deacon's stole.

## Surgery

### Thursday 9th August 2001

The surgery took longer than anticipated because Jack's lower spine was so badly ruptured, and was further complicated by a significant tearing of the dura mater (the membrane surrounding the spinal cord, housing protective fluids). As it was badly torn, much of the fluids leaked out causing the protruding bony areas to rub against the spinal cord itself.

Dr Banco was most surprised that Jack had managed to survive throughout the summer of 2001. During the consultation following the operation he told Jack that it was amazing that his spine had not been seriously damaged and that he could even walk.

### Saturday 11th August 2001

This was the anniversary of Newman's death in 1890. Jack was told to lie in bed perfectly still on his left side in order to allow the incision in the dura to heal. The pain was so severe that morphine had to be administered every few hours. "I remember that at the time my heart was filled with joy and gratitude to Cardinal Newman for seeing me through this difficult surgery."

### Tuesday 14th August 2001

Jack was told that he could not be discharged from hospital until he was able to walk with the aid of a walking stick. The pain was still extremely intense every time he moved or shifted his position in bed. As a result he was not able to sleep either during the day or the night.

During the late morning, after he had received his medication to relieve the pain, Jack's physiotherapist came into his room and announced that it was time for a walking test. "I wondered how I would be able to walk when even to move to the edge of the bed was agony. The physiotherapist gave me a walker and I somehow managed to get out of bed. The pain was so severe that after a short time I had to be helped back onto the bed by two attendants. To make matters worse I was told that my recovery period would be extended by several months. I was demoralised."

## Healing

### Wednesday 15th August 2001

Jack Sullivan's wonderful healing, now accepted as a miracle by the Catholic Church, took place during the following day, Wednesday 15th August 2001, the Feast of the Assumption. Jack has told the deeply moving and inspirational story in his own words (p. 15 above).

## Thursday 16th August 2001

The following day the nurse who visited Jack at his home was surprised to find him virtually pain free. When he had been discharged from hospital the previous day the doctor had advised Jack to sleep on the ground floor so that he did not have to climb the stairs to his bedroom on the second floor. The nurse recommended that he walk for short distances in his garden but that he should be careful about bending.

## Sunday 19th August 2001

Instead of having Holy Communion brought to him by the Pastoral Associate of St Christine's Parish, in Marshfield, Massachusetts, Jack was able to attend the 9:00am Mass - standing up straight. The congregation was amazed and astounded to see Jack Sullivan standing upright and walking normally, as they knew of the severity of his condition and recent surgery. The last time he had entered the church he was hunched over with his face looking towards the ground.

## Monday 20th August 2001

Jack began walking further and found he could walk from a quarter of a mile to more than a mile each day without the aid of a walking stick. Within another two weeks Jack was able to walk more than two miles each day, and has done so ever since. He felt amazingly fit. He telephoned Dr Banco.

After describing his condition, Jack asked Dr Banco's permission to return to the internship programme. He was thrilled when Dr Banco enthusiastically agreed that he could return to the programme and wished him well.

**Thursday 23rd August 2001**

After Jack had been at home for eight days Dr Banco allowed him to finish his 25 hours of remaining internship. Jack went to the Chaplain's office at the Brigham Hospital. Everyone he met was astounded by his remarkable and speedy recovery, standing up straight and walking comfortably.

**Tuesday 11th September 2001**

The Programme Director and Assistant Director asked Jack to attend a meeting at the Seminary prior to his return to classes for the fourth and final year of his Diaconate Formation. Given the difficulties Jack had experienced that summer at the Brigham Hospital, they had serious concerns about allowing him to continue, thinking it would be too strenuous. They did not know the details of Jack's recovery. To get to the office Jack had to climb four flights of stairs.

"I bounded up those stairs while the Assistant Director stood at the top, looking down. She kept telling me to slow down. When she and the Programme Director saw me in their office, standing straight and without any pain, they quickly changed their minds. In mid-September 2001, I returned to classes and also full-time to my work at Plymouth Court. Everyone was amazed and thrilled by what God had done for me."

**Wednesday 3rd October 2001**

Jack went to his post-operative review meeting with Dr Banco: "He anticipated my recovery to take up to three months, not a few days. After a thorough examination he exclaimed that he had no medical or scientific explanation for my remarkable recovery."

Dr Banco told Jack: "Your recovery is unbelievable, 100 per cent and totally remarkable. I have never seen a healing process occur so quickly and so completely. You have the bending and lifting capacity of a 30-year-old man."

Jack then asked Dr Banco the all-important question and one that he had been wrestling with for more than two years. This particular question would confirm Jack's feelings about Cardinal Newman's intercession on his behalf. He asked Dr Banco if he could give him a medical explanation as to why the pain had stopped throughout the eight months of his third year of studies to become a Permanent Deacon; and also why the pain had suddenly disappeared on 15th August 2001, the last day that he was in the hospital.

Dr Banco responded: "Jack, I have absolutely no medical explanation to give you as to why your pain stopped. The MRI scans and the subsequent intrusive surgery confirmed the severity of your spinal condition. With the tear in your dura mater your condition should have been much worse. I have no medical or scientific answer for you. If you want an answer, ask God."

In tears, Jack Sullivan realised that Dr Banco had just confirmed to him what he had suspected for the past two years. "I decided to write a letter to Father Paul Chavasse, Postulator of the Newman Cause, at the Birmingham Oratory, because God's purpose for all of this, I thought, was the Beatification of Cardinal Newman."

## LIFE SINCE

### Ordination as a Permanent Deacon

Jack's ordination as a Permanent Deacon was put back a week because Cardinal Bernard Law, Archbishop of Boston, was away in Rome. The Ordination was re-scheduled for Saturday 14th September 2002, the Feast of the Triumph of the Cross and took place at the Cathedral of the Holy Cross in Boston.

Something also happened on that day that Jack will never forget: "A special sign of the kindly intercession of Cardinal Newman occurred. I had always prayed for Cardinal Newman's intercession, not to be healed for I felt that would be too presumptuous, but to enable me to return to classes in both my third and fourth year and that I be ordained a deacon. Father Paul Chavasse notified Father Drew Morgan, Provost of the Pittsburgh Oratory in Pennsylvania, via e-mail that he and others involved in the Cause for Cardinal Newman's Beatification had concluded that my healing was worthy of further investigation. Father Chavasse asked Father Morgan to notify me of this fact as soon as possible. As a result of his decision, Father Paul Chavasse planned to take my letter to Rome. At the time, Father Chavasse had no idea that I was being ordained to the Diaconate in Boston on the same day that he sent his e-mail. It was a truly wonderful sign from God."

Jack Sullivan's recovery has remained permanent and complete since 15th August 2001, the day he was discharged from hospital in Boston. Each summer Jack has undertaken tough work including digging in his vegetable gardens and flowerbeds. "Since my surgery, my recovery has remained permanent and complete. I am able to undertake rigorous work in the garden of our house including raking leaves on our acre of lawn. I also dig and cultivate the flower and vegetable gardens, often lifting large rocks. The summer following my healing I built a brick wall two feet high and twenty feet long. Often I have to lift sixty-pound bags of fertiliser, peat moss and topsoil. During 2006 we moved into our new courthouse in Plymouth during which I lifted heavy boxes and equipment with absolutely no ill effects." He has had no difficulties in what he has to do in his work at Plymouth

Court or in his ministry as a Permanent Deacon at his assigned parish of St Thecla in Pembroke, Massachusetts.

**Prison ministry**

Jack is very involved in prison ministry due to his affiliation with Courts, law-enforcement and his knowledge of prison facilities: "Prison ministry came naturally to me. I have come to know what motivates inmates and how they think. While in formation I expressed a desire to engage in prison ministry, but the Archdiocese automatically assigns deacons to parishes so prison work seemed untenable. But, despite this, I was eventually assigned to work in the prison. I have been designated to co-ordinate the Catholic Chaplaincy at Plymouth prison by the Archdiocese of Boston and am assisted by about 15 Extraordinary Ministers of Holy Communion, another deacon and four priests.

"I also present RCIA (Adult Catechetical Classes) for inmates every Monday evening from September to April, preparing them for the Sacraments of Baptism and Confirmation. It is a most worthwhile and rewarding ministry.

"Despite all the pain and anxiety that I have experienced throughout these eventful years it has been a deeply spiritual and enriching experience. As a result I have tried to develop a greater degree of trust and confidence in God's merciful providence, surrendering myself to His will day by day."

## Proclamation of the Decree

The great news arrived from Rome on Friday 3rd July 2009, the Feast of St Thomas, the Apostle. The announcement was released in a bulletin by the Vatican Press Office at noon (local time). The English version read:

*Decrees of the Congregation for the Causes of Saints*

*Today, during a private audience with Archbishop Angelo Amato SDB, Prefect of the Congregation for the Causes of Saints, the Pope authorised the Congregation to promulgate a number of decrees, among them the following:*
*MIRACLES*
*-Servant of God John Henry Newman, English Cardinal and Founder of the Oratories of St Philip Neri in England (1801-1890).*

The miracle necessary for the beatification of the Venerable John Henry Cardinal Newman (1801-1890), probably the best-known English churchman in Victorian England, had been approved by the Cardinals and prelates of the Vatican Congregation for the Causes of Saints on Tuesday 2nd June 2009.

**John Henry Newman.**

## Beatus

Beatification comes from the Latin word *beatus*, meaning happy, blessed, holy. Beatification is an act by which the Catholic Church, through an official decree by the Pope, permits public veneration under the title Blessed, of a dead person whose life is marked by holiness and the heroic practice of the virtues.

## "My Intercessor and Special Friend."

This author telephoned Jack Sullivan and gave him the joyful news. Asked for his initial reaction Jack responded by email 24 hours later: "When I first learned of the favourable recommendation of the Cardinal and bishops, I felt a sense of awe and immense gratitude to God and Cardinal Newman.

"If it wasn't for Cardinal Newman's intercession when I was experiencing extremely severe spinal problems, it would have been virtually impossible to complete my diaconate formation and be ordained for the Archdiocese of Boston. Nor would I have been able to continue in my chosen profession as a magistrate in our court system to support my family.

"My fervent desire to give all that I have in my parish ministry at both St Thecla's parish in Pembroke, Massachusetts, and my prison ministry at the House of Correction in Plymouth, Massachusetts, best expresses the intense appreciation I have for God's gift and Cardinal Newman, who directs my efforts.

"I have developed a very real relationship with Cardinal Newman in frequent prayer and I try to pass on what marvellous gifts I have received to those I meet. Secondly, when receiving the news, I felt a very deep sense of the reality of God's love for each one of us, especially during times of immense difficulties and suffering.

"I realise that indeed there is such a thing as the Communion of Saints and a place of perfect peace which God has prepared for each one of us. As the kindly light of truth guided the life of Newman amidst unspeakable challenges in his world, so too I feel the same sense of direction when reflecting on these awesome gifts by realising that God dispenses His favour especially on the lowly and those who are ordinary as beautifully described in Our Lady's praises in her Magnificat."

At the time that Pope Benedict authorised the promulgation of the Decree, Jack Sullivan and his wife Carol had never visited either England or Rome. In a subsequent email to this author Jack added: "Carol and I very much look forward to visiting the Birmingham Oratory and other places connected with Cardinal Newman. In particular, I wish to come close to him, the person that I most admire, by visiting the Oratory he founded, his room and his chapel, and by standing before the grave where he was buried.

"The writings of Cardinal Newman are so relevant today in view of our tendencies towards intellectualism and lack of doctrine, in this secular age in which we live during the early part of the 21st century."

Jack Sullivan added: "I decided to pray for Cardinal Newman's intercession when afflicted with my serious back problems. At that time it seemed very unlikely I would be allowed to return to my classes for the third and fourth years. The following morning after my prayer the night before, all the pain disappeared, enabling me to walk and return to classes. Since that moment Newman has become a significant part of my life. I pray to Cardinal Newman every morning: *'Good morning, Cardinal Newman, my intercessor and special friend'.*"

## Pope Benedict XVI and Cardinal Newman

In April 1990 Cardinal Ratzinger had described Newman as "the great English Cardinal", at a special Audience with Pope John Paul II for delegates attending a Newman Symposium, organised by the international Centre of Newman Friends, in Rome.

Introducing the delegates, Cardinal Ratzinger said: "Newman Scholars and Newman Friends from various countries, as well as professors and students from many Universities in Rome and elsewhere, have met in these days in the Eternal City to celebrate in a fitting way the Centenary of the death of the great English Cardinal, John Henry Newman." He also mentioned how, as a seminarian, he was first introduced to the writings of Newman at the age of eighteen.

In welcoming John Paul II, he continued: "Holy Father, over the years of your pontificate you have repeatedly evoked the name of John Henry Newman as a spiritual father and inspiring master on the way to holiness and as a secure guide in the search for eternal truth."

In turn, Pope John Paul II began his address: "I welcome all of you and thank you for drawing attention through your celebration to the great English Cardinal's special place in the history of the Church. The passage of a hundred years since his death has done nothing to diminish the importance of this extraordinary figure, many of whose ideas enjoy a particular relevance in our own day."

**Newman among the great teachers of the Church**

Cardinal Joseph Ratzinger, during his introduction to the third day of the Newman Symposium in Rome on 28th April 1990, said: "Today's third and final day of our Newman Symposium is devoted to the echo that Newman's figure and work found, first at that time - one hundred years ago - and then, in the theology of the present time. Perhaps it is meaningful and in accord with the theme of this day if I tell a little about my own way to Newman, in which indeed something is reflected of the presence of this great English theologian in the intellectual and spiritual struggle of our time.

"In January 1946, when I began my study of theology in the Seminary in Freising which had finally reopened after the problems of the war, an older student was assigned as prefect to our group. Alfred Lapple had begun to work on a dissertation on Newman's theology of conscience even before the beginning of the war. In all the years of his military service he had not lost sight of this theme, which he now turned to with new enthusiasm and energy. Soon we were bonded by a personal friendship, wholly centred on the great problems of philosophy and theology. Newman was always present to us."

Later in his introduction, Cardinal Ratzinger went on: "When I continued my studies in Munich in 1947, I found a well-read and enthusiastic follower of Newman in the Fundamental Theologian, Gottlieb Sohngen, who was my true teacher in theology. He opened up the *Grammar of Assent* to us and in doing so, the special manner and form of certainty in religious knowledge.

"... Here the figure of St Augustine comes to my mind, with whom Newman was so associated... Newman had written his own experience of a never finished conversion and interpreted for us, not only the way of Christian doctrine, but also that of the Christian life. The characteristic of the great doctor of the Church, it seems to me, is that he teaches not only through his thought and speech, but also rather by his life, because within him thought and life are interpenetrated and defined. If this is so, then Newman belongs to the great teachers of the Church, because at the same time he touches our hearts and enlightens our thinking."

### Canonisation

After Cardinal Joseph Ratzinger was elected Bishop of Rome and Successor of St Peter in the Sistine Chapel, on Tuesday 19th April 2005, this author raised the question: Will it be Benedict XVI, the first Pope of the twenty-first century, who will canonise John Henry Newman, and declare him a Doctor of the Church? Except for the martyrs,

Newman would be the first English saint to be canonised since well before the Reformation. (*Benedict XVI and Cardinal Newman*).

St Thomas Cantilupe of Hereford, (1218-82), was the last Englishman canonised before the Reformation. He died at Ferento, near Orvieto, in Italy on the 25th August 1282. He was buried in Hereford Cathedral and, with his canonisation during the Pontificate of Pope John XXII in 1320, his shrine became a popular place of pilgrimage.

Meanwhile, at the time of the promulgation of the Decree, opinion was divided as to the venue for the beatification ceremony between a location in Rome or in the Archdiocese of Birmingham. The norm during the Pontificate of Benedict XVI has been for beatification ceremonies to take place in the diocese where the Servant of God lived and died.

The two main reasons put forward for having the ceremony in Rome were: firstly, the world-wide interest in Cardinal Newman both as a theologian and writer but also as a holy, humble and pastoral parish priest who looked after the sick and poor of his Oratory Parish in Edgbaston. Secondly, the fact that Newman is a Cardinal of the Holy Roman Church. When he was created a Cardinal by Pope Leo XIII in 1879, Newman requested permission to continue to live and work in Birmingham rather than move to Rome, as was the norm for Cardinals at that time. The

Pope granted permission and Cardinal Newman died at the Oratory House in Edgbaston on Monday 11th August 1890.

*POSTSCRIPT*

Archbishop Vincent Nichols, Archbishop of Westminster and President of the Catholic Bishops' Conference of England and Wales, Bishop William Kenney, CP, Diocesan Administrator in the Archdiocese of Birmingham, and Fr Paul Chavasse, Provost of the Birmingham Oratory and Actor of the Newman Cause, met at Archbishop's House, Westminster, on Tuesday 21st July, to discuss possible dates and a venue for the beatification ceremony of Cardinal Newman.

The beatification ceremony will be held in the Archdiocese of Birmingham, on a Sunday, probably during late May or early June 2010. No official announcement will be made until both date and venue have been approved by the Holy See.

The Roman summer holiday had already began as this booklet went to the printer on Friday 31st July, and an official announcement from the Secretariat of State about the beatification ceremony is unlikely before late September 2009 at the earliest.

Jack Sullivan, as he had first done nine years before, contacted Father Paul Chavasse at the Birmingham Oratory. This time it was a simple message: "I volunteer to serve as a deacon during Mass at the beatification ceremony of Cardinal Newman."

## A Meditation by Cardinal Newman

God has created me to do him some definite service; he has committed some work to me which he has not committed to another. I have my mission - I may never know it in this life, but I shall be told it in the next.

I am a link in a chain, a bond of connection between persons. He has not created me for naught. I shall do good, I shall do his work; I shall be an angel of peace, a preacher of truth in my own place, while not intending it, if I do but keep his commandments and serve him in my calling.

Therefore I will trust him. Whatever, wherever I am, I can never be thrown away. If I am in sickness, my sickness may serve him; in perplexity, my perplexity may serve him; if I am in sorrow, my sorrow may serve him. My sickness, or perplexity, or sorrow may be necessary causes of some great end, which is quite beyond us. He does nothing in vain; he may prolong my life, he may shorten it; he knows what he is about. He may take away my friends, he may throw me among strangers, he may make me feel desolate, make my spirits sink, hide my future from me - still he knows what he is about.

(*Meditations and Devotions*, written by Cardinal Newman during the 1850s for the boys of the Oratory School, published in 1893. This is taken from 'Meditations on Christian Doctrine').

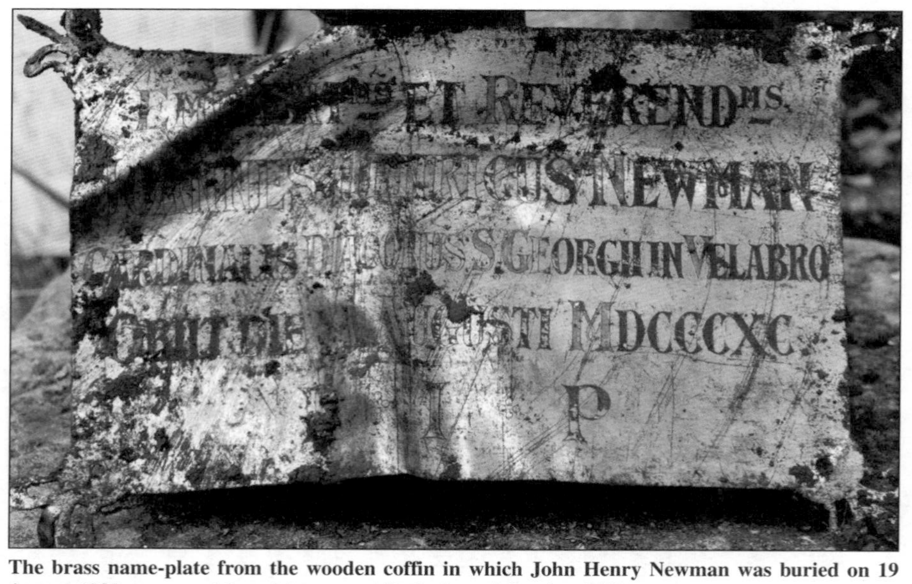


**The brass name-plate from the wooden coffin in which John Henry Newman was buried on 19 August 1890, recovered from his grave at Rednal, on 2 October 2008.**

## Recommended further reading

*Benedict XVI and Cardinal Newman*, Edited by Peter Jennings, (Family Publications, Oxford, 2005).
*John Henry Newman - In His Time*, (Family Publications, Oxford, 2007).
*John Henry Newman*, A Biography, Ian Ker, (re- issue, OUP, 2009).

## Acknowledgements

I owe a great debt of gratitude to the Fathers of the Birmingham Oratory, founded by Cardinal Newman; in particular to the late Fr Stephen Dessain, to Fr Gregory Winterton, and to his successor as Provost, Fr Paul Chavasse.

I am most grateful to Archbishop Vincent Nichols, now Archbishop of Westminster, whom I have known since September 1980, for his Foreword. To Abbot Cuthbert Johnson OSB, now chaplain at St Mary's Abbey, Oulton, Staffordshire; to my wife Stella Jennings who typed Deacon Jack Sullivan's original handwritten manuscript; and to Kevin Grant for his help and encouragement; also to Fergal Martin, General Secretary of the Catholic Truth Society.

Most of all, I should like to thank Jack and Carol Sullivan who gave Fr Chavasse and me generous hospitality in their home during the two visits we made to Boston, Massachusetts, in July and November 2006. My thanks also go to Brian, Jennifer and Jessica, their grown-up children, for their welcome and kindness.

## About the author

Peter Jennings is a Catholic journalist, writer, broadcaster, and public relations consultant. He has written and broadcast extensively on the Catholic Church and the Vatican since the late 1970s and began working with the Fathers of the Birmingham Oratory on the Newman Cause in 1975. His book *Benedict XVI and Cardinal Newman* (Family Publications, Oxford) was launched at the English College in Rome during October 2005. He was Press Secretary to the now Archbishop of Westminster, Vincent Nichols, during the latter's nine years as Archbishop of Birmingham, 2000-2009. He contributes to The Times *Register* and writes regularly for Times Online.

**Picture credits**

Cover: Original 19th century photograph of Father John Henry Newman taken c 1865 by R W Thrupp of Birmingham. Page 6: Original photograph of Newman as a Father of the Birmingham Oratory, taken c 1870 by Draycott of London & Birmingham. Both pictures given to Pope Benedict XVI by Prime Minister, Rt Hon Tony Blair, MP at a Private Audience in the Vatican on 23 June 2007. Page 52: Original photograph of Dr Newman taken c 1866 by McLean & Haes Photographs, London. All from the Archives of the Birmingham Oratory, courtesy of the Fathers. Cover, Pages 16 and 32: Deacon Jack Sullivan; name-plate from Cardinal Newman's coffin, Page 62, pictures by Peter Jennings.

# Behold, His Yeshua!

# Behold, His Yeshua!

Psalm 91

JEFFREY D. JOHNSON

Foreword by Nicole Y. Yoder

RESOURCE *Publications* • Eugene, Oregon

BEHOLD, HIS YESHUA!
Psalm 91



Resource Publications
An Imprint of Wipf and Stock Publishers
199 W. 8th Ave., Suite 3
Eugene, OR 97401

www.wipfandstock.com

PAPERBACK ISBN: 978-1-7252-8427-2
HARDCOVER ISBN: 978-1-7252-8428-9
EBOOK ISBN: 978-1-7252-8429-6

Manufactured in the U.S.A. JULY 13, 2020

For Louise, my anchor of true faith and courage,
and a true woman of God.

## PRAYER FOR HEALTH

By Rabbi Chaim Yosef David Azulai (1724–1806)

Master of the Universe: With Your compassion, grant us the physical strength, health, and ability so that we may function effectively, and may we experience no illness or pain. Enable us to serve You in joy, contentment, and health. Save us from all evil and prolong our days in goodness and our years in sweetness. Enrich our years and add to our days and years of dedicated service to You. Shield us in the shadow of Your wings and spare us and all our family from all harsh or evil decrees. May we be at rest and calm, vigorous, and fresh to serve and revere You.

# Contents

# Foreword

THROUGHOUT THE AGES, THE Psalms have been the worship book of both church and synagogue. The prayers and songs recorded there teach us much about the character of God and how to approach Him. From them, we also experience solace in time of trouble and are inspired to praise our Creator.

Few Psalms, however, are as beloved as Psalm 91. Through it, we are reminded of the amazing truth that when we make the Almighty our dwelling place, whatever trials may come, we are protected, and we do not face them alone. We can also rest assured that God's purposes will always be fulfilled even in (or despite) the snares and strategies of the evil one. The cultural and Hebrew insights deftly woven throughout this meditation add new depth of understanding; and the prayers of the saints throughout the ages remind us of that great cloud of witnesses who have run the race before. From them, the reader may glean wisdom.

These days, as the world is facing a health and economic crisis, the encouragement found in this devotional is timely, as is the challenge toward increased trust and intimacy with our Heavenly Father. Through the discipline of prayer and the meditation on the truths in this

Psalm highlighted so beautifully by Dr. Johnson, one may indeed find an anchor for the soul.

Nicole Y. Yoder

VP Aid and Aliyah, International Christian Embassy Jerusalem; M.A. Judeo-Christian Synergism, Master's International University of Divinity; M.A. International Community Development, Northwest University

# Preface

*Behold, His Yeshua!* was written during the beginning of the pandemic of 2019–20. This pandemic and its disease brought about great fear and despair.

Over a period of several weeks, this nine-part series was emailed to Israel Today Ministries' constituency and put on social media. The response was awe-inspiring. Requests came for a booklet to become available. Here it is. No claim is made for originality, but the writer is deeply grateful for the help he received from many sources, including those in the bibliography found in the back of this booklet.

May your heart be strengthened, full of peace, and have great certainty about God's protection as you reflect upon the words of this profound psalm.

Jeffrey D. Johnson, May 2020
www.israeltodayministries.org
Facebook.com/IsraelTodayMinistries
Twitter: @drjeffitm

PART ONE

# No Need to Fear

## Psalm 91:1

*He who dwells in the shelter of the Most High will abide in the shadow of the Almighty" (v. 1).*

PSALM 91 SPEAKS OF God's protection from dangers and things like plagues. The Talmud refers to Psalm 91 as *The Song of Plagues* (Shev Shema'tata 15b). This psalm might have been sung by two people antiphonally—there is a *profound paused ending* where God speaks in verses 14–16.

This psalm is read in the synagogue on Saturday mornings and at the close of the evening services on Saturday night and at funeral services. I personally end my official letters and notes with my signature and Psalm 91.

Traditional Jewish thought is that **Moses wrote** Psalm 91 during the wilderness wanderings, and that David compiled the psalm and added it to his book of psalms. Whether the author is Moses or David, the psalm is profound.

## THE PSALM IS WONDERFUL TO MEDITATE UPON AND TO PRAY BACK TO GOD

"He who dwells in the shelter (Hebrew: *sayther*—cover) of the Most High *(Elyon)* will abide in the shadow (Hebrew: *tsale*—shade) of the Almighty (*Shaddai)*" (v. 1).

*Shelter. . .shade* literally means "secret hiding place." Believers feel protected from pursuing enemies (Ps. 31:20–21). This protectiveness comes from the reality found in Genesis 19:8 where the "men" found "shelter or shade" in Lot's home from the pursuing enemies. Even today, with Bedouins, and generally throughout the Middle East, those who enter their homes come under their "shade" or protection. The idea of great hospitality, protection, and provision comes from the Hebrew word *Hesed* often translated "mercy."

*Shaddai* and *Elyon* are ancient names of God. God revealed the name *Shaddai* (Almighty) to Abraham (Exod. 6:3) before He revealed His unspeakable name of *YHVH* (Exod. 3:14; 15:3). Rather than attempting to pronounce *YHVH*, as many Christians do, Jews will say, *Adonai* or *HaShem*.

## POINTS TO PONDER

1. Believers are in the "shade" of the Almighty.
2. We are protected from harm and from anything or anyone pursuing us.
3. God will never abandon His children.

4. There is no need to fear; He will help us (Heb. 13:5–6; Isa. 41:13).

Read and meditate upon the verses mentioned in this brief devotional.

When tempted to fear, remember what God said in verse one, and like a child, reach up and take hold of His hand and feel safe in His "shade" and protection.

## PRAYER

We beseech thee, Master, to be our helper and protector.
Save the afflicted among us; have mercy on the lowly;
Raise up the fallen; appear to the needy; heal the ungodly;
Restore the wanderers of thy people;
Feed the hungry; ransom our prisoners;
Raise up the sick; comfort the faint-hearted.

Clement of Rome (1st Century)

## PART TWO

# You are the Temple!

## Psalms 91:2–4

*"I will say to the* LORD *(Adonai), 'My refuge and my fortress, My God (Elohi[m]), in whom I trust'" (v. 2).*

*REFUGE* AND *FORTRESS* ARE very strong expressions indicating that God is sovereign, the ruler of the universe.

*Shelter of the Most High* (v. 1) and *refuge, fortress* (v. 2) are references to the Temple where the presence of God dwelt. As dangers from demons, war, wild beasts, and plagues do exist and do happen to believers, protection, security, and peace were found within the Temple. "For in the day of trouble He will conceal me in His tabernacle; In the secret place of His tent He will hide me; He will lift me up on a rock" (Ps. 27:5).

Within the psalm there is an interchange of first and second persons (first person: I/We; second person: You). God directly speaks in verses 14–16.

> *"For it is He who delivers you from the snare of the trapper and from the deadly pestilence" (v. 3).*

The second person speaks. *Trapper* refers to the fowler, the one who entraps birds. The implication is that God will protect you from the dangerous attempts against your life that comes from evil, pestilence, famine, et.al.

> *"He will cover you with His pinions, and under His wings you may seek refuge; His faithfulness is a shield and bulwark" (v.4).*

This is the verse I use when I sign letters and correspondence, I write:

Shalom and Blessings,
Until He comes, we are
Together Under His Wings,

*Pinions* is a reference to a bird spreading its wings over its young in the nest protecting, shielding, covering, hiding them from potential danger.

*Under His wings* according to Rashi (1040–1105) is the Shekinah (Divine Presence of God). Believers rest in His shadow, for God protects him. The wings may also refer to the cherubim on either side of the Ark (Exod. 25:17–22). The Divine Presence hovered over the Ark.

*Shield*: A shield could in fact completely surround and protect the warrior. The Talmud suggests it was a shield that moved round about him (Ibn Ezra and Targum).

*Bulwark*: A bulwark is a wall, a barricade, protection, and defense against attack.

Both shield and bulwark are an encompassing shield of protection.

## POINTS TO PONDER:

1. God is sovereign, the ruler of the universe.
2. Believers are under the Divine Presence of God.
3. God's protection is an encompassing shield.
4. The Temple, where the presence of God dwells, is where you find safety and peace.
5. For those of you who are believers in Jesus remember Paul's words: "*Your body is the temple of the Holy Spirit who is in you, whom you have from God, and you are not your own? For you were bought at a price; therefore, glorify God in your body and in your spirit, which are God's*" (1 *Cor.* 6:19–20 *(NKJV)).*
6. The peace, protection, and safety we all long for is found in Jesus. The presence of God, through the Holy Spirit, dwells in you. We need not fear.

> *". . .In the world, you will have tribulation; but be of good cheer, I have overcome the world" (John* 16:33 *(NKJV)).*
>
> *"Peace I leave with you, My peace I give to you; not as the world gives do I give to you. Let not your heart be troubled, neither let it be afraid" (John* 14:27 *(NKJV)).*

## PRAYER

Lord, because you have made me, I owe you the whole of my love;
because you have redeemed me, I owe you the whole of myself;
because you have promised so much, I owe you my whole being.

Moreover, I owe you as much more love than myself as you are greater than I,
for whom you gave yourself and to whom you promised yourself.
I pray you, Lord, make me taste by love what I taste by knowledge;
let me know by love what I know by understanding.
I owe you more than my whole self, but I have no more,
and by myself I cannot render the whole of it to you.
Draw me to you, Lord, in the fullness of your love.
I am wholly yours by creation; make me all yours, too, in love.

—Anselm (AD 1033–1109)

PART THREE

# Deadly Sandstorms

## *What Happens in the Darkness?*

Psalm 91:5–6

*"You will not be afraid of the terror by night, or of the arrow that flies by day; of the pestilence that stalks in darkness, or of the destruction that lays waste at noon" (vv. 5–6).*

*TERROR BY NIGHT* IS the absence of light. In the light, you can see and understand. However, in the darkness, just as today, ancient folklore told of demons and evil spirits who lurked in the opaque atmosphere of night. When you are alone at night, not knowing who or what is out there, you need not fear, for God will protect your soul and your being.

*Arrow that flies by day* is not a human weapon, rather, metaphorically some demonic power. "The LORD will protect you from all evil: He will keep your soul. The

LORD will guard your going out and your coming in from this time forth and forever" (Ps. 121:7–8; cf. Song 3:8).

*Pestilence*: The context is that of demons or envoys of evil.

*Destruction*: The Hebrew word is *qetev* meaning "destroying, to cut-off, to scourge" like that of a scorching desert wind or a deadly sandstorm.

## POINTS TO PONDER

1. God protects in the darkness, where there is no light, and at noon, when the brightest of the light shines.
2. Jesus taught his disciples, "What I tell you in the darkness, speak in the light; and what you hear whispered in your ear, proclaim upon the housetops" (Matt. 10:27).
3. It is in the darkness that we learn to listen to Jesus. It is during the times of trial and uncertain circumstances that He whispers in our ears.
4. To hear Him, we must be quiet. If we talk or move around busying ourselves with "helps," we may not hear. Be silent and pause.
5. Listen to what God wants to say through the Holy Spirit, and then, in the light, shout it from the rooftops or simply share with your neighbor or loved one.
6. Through the discipline, we learn that in the darkness humility comes and our hearts grow into clay from stone, and then we can hear God.

## PRAYER

Lord, thou hast given us thy Word for a light to shine upon our path; grant us so to meditate on that Word, and to follow its teaching, that we may find in it the light that shines more and more until the perfect day, through Jesus Christ our Lord.

—Jerome (ca. AD 342–420)

PART FOUR

# Come, and See!

## Psalm 91:7–8

*"A thousand may fall at your side and ten thousand at your right hand, but it shall not approach you. You will only look on with your eyes and see the recompense of the wicked" (vv.7–8).*

*At your side* is referencing the left side, as compared to the right (hand) side. It is a Hebraic poetic nuance. The right hand emphasizes strength.

*It* is referring to the "arrow" in verse 5, the pestilence, the envoys of evil and destruction.

*Shall not approach you* comforts us in knowing that we who believe and trust in God will be secure. Multitudes who do not have God's protection, because of their unbelief, will fall around us. However, believers need not worry.

*Your eyes. . .see*: Because no harm comes to the believer, they will see the wicked defeated with their very own eyes. With their own eyes, they will see God's power.

Jesus said, "Come, and. . .see" (John 1:39). Andrew said to Simon, "We have found the Messiah" (John 1:41). To "come" is an act of faith. Faith opens one's eyes to see the Messiah.

The enemy attacks us all. "When the devil had finished every temptation, he left Him until an opportune time" (Luke 4:13). Satan tempted Jesus for forty days in the wilderness, but Jesus defeated Satan by quoting Scripture. Satan left Him for a season "until an opportune time," which was during the agony of Gethsemane.

> "Then He said to them, 'My soul is deeply grieved, to the point of death; remain here and keep watch with Me.' And He went a little beyond them, and fell on His face and prayed, saying, 'My Father, if it is possible, let this cup pass from Me; yet not as I will, but as You will.'. . .He went away again a second time and prayed, saying, 'My Father, if this cannot pass away unless I drink it, Your will be done.'. . .And He left them again, and went away and prayed a third time, saying the same thing once more." (Matt. 26:38–39, 42, and 44).

Satan's final onslaught against Jesus as the "Son of Man" was at Gethsemane. "Son of Man" is a messianic term which implies His humanity, in contrast to the term "Son of God" which implies His divinity. Jesus was both fully "human" and fully "God."

The *cup* refers to His approaching death (Matt. 20:22). His humanity struggled and was tested in the garden. He was about to taste the pungent filth in the cup of death for the sin of the world.

*If this cup may not pass away. . .thy will be done* is a Greek nuance that something is determined as fulfilled, that, it is *true*. The Son of Man acquiesced to the Father's will fulfilling His destiny as the Son of God who became the Passover lamb, the Savior of the world. He made it possible for sinners to become sons (Greek: *tekna*—children) of God. His agony, His test, His moment of surrender was the beginning of our salvation. The crucifixion was the victory of the Son of Man over Satan's test.

His submission at Gethsemane surrendering to the fact that He was to die and become the "Sin Offering," the sacrifice, to save humanity from sin, changed humanity's compass forever. *Gethsemane* means "oil press" indicating the Son of Man was pressed into submission ("His sweat became like drops of blood" (Luke 22:44)) to the will of the Father. As a result, every person can now enter the presence of God because of what the Son of Man did. Through Jesus, anyone can "Come, and. . .see."

## POINTS TO PONDER:

1. Satan attacks us all. Jesus was attacked.
2. The Lord prayed three times before complete surrender to the Father's will. Paul prayed three times to the Lord about a "thorn in the flesh." God said no, that His grace was sufficient (2 Cor. 12:7–10). There were two attempts to heal the blind man at Bethsaida (Mark 8:22–25). When the trials come, believers pray. Sometimes the answer comes swiftly, and at times slowly, but an answer will come—either yes or no.

3. Jesus has made it possible for our redemption and peace.
4. We are not victims; we are conquerors.
5. People who haven't learned how to love often have a victim's mentality.
6. People who love do not feel limited. "Because he has loved Me, therefore I will deliver him" (Ps. 91:14).

## PRAYER

O Lord, who hast mercy upon all, take away
from me my sins,
and mercifully kindle in me the fire of thy Holy
Spirit.
Take away from me the heart of stone,
and give me a heart of flesh,
a heart to love and adore thee,
a heart to delight in thee,
to follow and to enjoy thee,
for Christ's sake.

—Ambrose of Milan (ca. AD 339–397)

PART FIVE

# Haven of Rest

## Psalm 91:9–10

*"For you have made the LORD, my refuge, even the Most High, your dwelling place. No evil will befall you, nor will any plague come near your tent" (vv. 9–10).*

*REFUGE* IS THE HEBREW word *"makseh"* which means refuge, or shelter from the storm, from danger of falsehood.

Another word translated "refuge" is found in Psalm 16:1—"Preserve me, O God, for I take refuge in You." This Hebrew word is *Chasithi* (Ka-see-tee) meaning "to seek refuge, to flee for protection, to put trust and hope in God." In Psalm 16, David was crying out to God for protection to guard him from evil. David was a man after God's own heart (1 Sam. 13:14; Acts 13:22). David's heart was joined with God's. David made many mistakes, from adultery to murder, and he knew that the enemy sought after his soul endeavoring to cause him to sin. He was saying that "I will put my trust in your protection, and I will put my trust in your truth—your Word is truth."

Sometimes we do things being misguided by our thoughts and our self-perceived spirituality. We justify things in our heart, only to find out later that we made the wrong choice and the ramifications were severe. David knew this experience and was reaching out to God for help. He did not want to wander from God's path.

> ". . .Even the Most High, your dwelling place. No evil will befall you, nor will any plague come near your tent."

The LXX (Septuagint: Greek Old Testament—Jews used this version principally at the time of Jesus) translates verses nine and ten this way, "For thou, O Lord, art my hope: Thou my soul, hast made the Most High thy refuge. No evils shall come upon thee, and no scourge shall draw nigh to thy dwelling."

The emphasis is a little clearer in the LXX. God's dwelling is on high—the "Most High" (Hebrew: *Elyon*)—and is out of reach for those "evils" pursuing you. God's protection is a "haven of rest." He is truly our "refuge" in troubled times.

## POINTS TO PONDER:

1. God does not keep us free from trouble.
2. When trouble comes, He gives us choices to make. The psalmist chose to make the "Most High" his refuge. We have a choice to run towards or run away from God during times of trial.

3. Our plans, our schemes, our strengths, and our failures are some of the things that seemingly would put a wedge between us and God.
4. Nothing can separate us from His love (Rom. 8:35–39).
5. Like David, we always can reach out to God who loves us and seek refuge in His haven, so that we do not wander away from His path.
6. Life without hardships and testing is impossible, whether in the flesh or the spirit.
7. God has given each of us free will. We choose.
8. Virtue, strength, and wisdom physically and spiritually are acquired.
9. We must discipline both body and spirit.
10. Resistance, testing, and difficulty strengthen both the body and the spirit. And all of us will experience these difficulties. When the enemy comes, remember the words of our Master: "These things I have spoken unto you, that in me ye might have peace. In the world ye shall have tribulation: but be of good cheer; I have overcome the world" (John 16:33).
11. Holiness, security, and peace unfolds as we trust in the protection and truth of the "Most High."

## PRAYER

We ask you, Master, be our helper and defender. Rescue those of our number in distress; raise up the fallen; assist the needy; heal the sick; turn back those of your people who stray; feed the hungry; release our captives; revive the weak; encourage those who lose heart. Let all the nations realize that you are the only God, that Jesus Christ is your Child, and that we are your people and the sheep of your pasture.

*—First Epistle of Clement (ca. AD 96)*

PART SIX

# Face to Face with God and Angels

## Psalm 91:11

*"For He will give His angels charge concerning you, to guard you in all your ways" (v. 11).*

*Angels* ARE LIKE DIVINE bodyguards. *Angel* (Hebrew: *malach*) means a "messenger" who communicates the king's wishes. An angel represents the king—God, the king. God sends angels to fulfil a specific task, a mission of God's choosing. The Talmud says that certain angels accompany a person throughout their life (Chagigah 16a). The Talmud is correct.

"Are they not all ministering spirits, sent out to render service for the sake of those who will inherit salvation?" (Heb. 1:14) This gives voice to the fact that angels not only serve Jesus (Matt. 4:11), but they also serve His children or "those who will inherit salvation."

> "See that you do not despise one of these little ones, for I say to you that their angels in heaven continually see the face of My Father who is in heaven" (Matt. 18:10).

*Face*: In Exodus 33:11, it is said that the LORD spoke with Moses face-to-face (Hebrew: *p'anim al p'anim).* Face to face is a very intimate position. When God spoke to Moses "face-to-face," it was a very intimate and other-worldly moment. In Matthew 18:10, Jesus warns those who would harm children and implies that judgment would be severe upon those who abuse. The angels assigned to little ones have intimate conversations with God face-to-face. He knows who harms the children.

*Guard you in all your ways* refers to protection from the evil onslaught of influences and attacks against God's people. *Ways* is the Hebrew word *derek* meaning one's journey, manner of one's course of life, or moral character, one's walk.

As evil attempts to persuade and dissuade our choices and our actions, angels will guard us as we walk. These divine bodyguards are protecting us from evil attack. In Daniel 10, the angel sent to Daniel with an answer was in battle with a satanic adversary. Michael, the prince of angels who watches over Israel (Dan. 12:1), came and helped defeat the adversary. Meanwhile, Daniel wrestled in prayer with no answer for twenty-one days. Though perhaps uncertain and tired, he kept "walking" in moral character and faith. The answer did come.

God Himself is sometimes camouflaged as an angel. "Now the LORD (YHVH) appeared to him by the [terebinths] of Mamre, while he was sitting at the tent door in the heat of the day. When he lifted up his eyes and looked, behold, three men were standing opposite him; and when he saw them, he ran from the tent door to meet them and bowed himself to the earth, and said, 'My Lord (*Adonai*), if now I have found favor in your sight, please do not pass your servant by'" (Gen. 18:1–3).

Abraham was sitting at the tent door in the heat of the day when three men appeared before him. Rabbinic scholars attest that he was still recovering from his circumcision (Gen. 17:24). Immediately, he recognized that one of the three was the Lord and the other two angels. Though in discomfort from the circumcision, he ran towards them and bowed before them, his face pressed in the earth. He washed their feet and brought food and drink, and he stood off to the side while they were eating. He knew who they were. After the meal, one of the angels said that Sarah would become pregnant and bear a son. She laughed. And the Lord asked, "Is anything too difficult for the Lord?" (Gen. 18:14) Or is anything too "marvelous for the Lord?"

## POINTS TO PONDER:

1. Our divine bodyguards (angels) fight for us.
2. Our angels have intimate conversations with God.
3. As we journey with God and trials come, even when we do not have immediate answers, we must persevere and keep walking until the answer comes.
4. Develop a sense of awe, reverence, and expectancy for the Lord's presence. There is no pretentiousness here, no artificial posturing. A developed sense of spiritual intuition acknowledges the Lord is in our midst.

5. Abraham's acts of humility, reverence, washing feet, and serving them is a mirror of what Jesus taught His disciples (John 13; Matt. 20:28). In times of trial or healing through pain, we are to serve and worship God—it's not about us; it's about Him.
6. As with Sarah, God knows our heart and how we often teeter questioning what He says. When pushed, we deny that we "laughed." Fear of the unknown often causes us to recoil. But then, low and behold, the miraculous happens.
7. God can do the impossible!

## PRAYER

> When you are alone, you should know that there is present with you the angel whom God has appointed for each man. . ..This angel, who is sleepless and cannot be deceived, is always present with you; he sees all things and is not hindered by darkness. You should know, too, that with him is God, who is in every place; for there is no place and nothing material in which God is not, since He is greater than all things and holds all men in His hand.
>
> —St. Anthony the Great (Anthony of Egypt, AD 251–356).

PART SEVEN

# Anxiety Fades; Satan Broken

Psalm 91:12–13

*"They will bear you up in their hands, that you do not strike your foot against a stone. You will tread upon the lion and cobra, the young lion and the serpent you will trample down" (vv.* 12–13*).*

*Your foot against a stone*: The context of the psalm emphasizes that angels carry us up in their hands and, as a result, we journey differently. The usual human troubles that come in life are faded, and we are spared.

*Lion and cobra* represent dangerous enemies, both physical and spiritual. The psalmist will overcome as angels protect him from the complexities and anxiety of the attack.

Both rabbinical and evangelical scholars submit that guardian angels protect God's people (Exod. 23:20; Psalm

34:7; 103:20; Matt. 18:10; Heb. 1:14). "Bless the LORD, you His angels, mighty in strength, who perform His word, obeying the voice of His word" (Psalm 103:20).

These two verses (Ps. 91:12–13) direct us to something, or should I say, to someone greater.

> "And he led Him to Jerusalem and had Him stand on the pinnacle of the temple, and said to Him, 'If You are the Son of God, throw Yourself down from here; for it is written, He will command His angels concerning You to guard You, and on their hands they will bear You up, so that You will not strike Your foot against a stone.' And Jesus answered and said to him, 'It is said, You shall not put the Lord Your God to the test.' When the devil had finished every temptation, he left Him" (Luke 4:9–13; cf. Matt. 4).

## SATAN USES THE SAME TEMPTATIONS HE USED WITH ADAM AND EVE.

1. *Temptation of the flesh:* You may eat of any tree (Gen. 3:1); If you are the Son of God, tell this stone to become bread (Luke 4:3).
2. *Temptation of private gain:* You will not die (Gen. 3:4); You will not hurt Your foot (Luke 4:11).
3. *Temptation of personal power:* You will be like God (Gen. 3:5); I will give you all this (Luke 4:5–6).

All temptations are wrapped up in these three points.

Had Jesus acquiesced to Satan's temptations He would have been yielding to a lesser power and would have nullified Himself as Messiah and Savior of the world.

Jesus highlights Psalm 91:13 to His disciples.

> "The seventy returned with joy, saying, 'Lord, even the demons are subject to us in Your name.' And He said to them, 'I was watching Satan fall from heaven like lightning. Behold, I have given you authority to tread on serpents and scorpions, and over all power of the enemy, and nothing will injure you. Nevertheless, do not rejoice in this, that the spirits are subject to you, but rejoice that your names are recorded in heaven'" (Luke 10: 17–20).

The disciples were elated they were victorious in their service to the Master. Jesus responded saying, "I was watching Satan fall from heaven like lightning." This does not mean that at that moment Satan was falling from heaven. Satan wishes he had the power of heaven (Isaiah 14:12–17), but he does not! Jesus was saying that Satan was falling from greatness and his dominion. His power had been broken, and in the Name of Jesus, Satan was brought to his knees, bowing before the authority of God the Son.

## POINTS TO PONDER:

1. Our walk is different as angels carry us in their hands.
2. Anxiety fades and complications diminish from the enemies' attacks because angels perform God's Word on our behalf.
3. Satan is brought to his knees before the authority of the name of Jesus.
4. We rejoice, not because of the deeds we do in service of the Lord, but rather we rejoice in the work that God does through us. It is all Him, not anything that

we do; therefore, we boast in Him and humbly praise Him that our "names are recorded in heaven."

## PRAYER

Let us think of the whole host of angels, how they stand by and serve his will, for Scriptures say: "Ten thousand times ten thousand were doing service to him, and they cried out: Holy, holy, holy, Lord Sabaoth; the whole of creation is full of His glory." Then let us gather together in awareness of our concord, as with one mouth we shout earnestly to him that we may become sharers in his great and glorious promises.

— Clement of Rome (ca. AD 96)

PART EIGHT

# You Know My Name!

## Psalm 91:14

*"Because he has loved Me, therefore I will deliver him; I will set him securely on high, because he has known My name" (v.14).*

WITHIN THE INITIAL PART of the psalm, there is a tradeoff discussion between first and second persons (first person: I/We; second person: You). The Targum, an Aramaic paraphrase and interpretation of the Hebrew Bible of the first century, suggests that the dialogue is between David and Solomon. Now in verses 14–16, God directly speaks.

*Because he has loved Me*: When someone loves another, self is completely diminished (Matt. 16:24), and one's sole purpose is to attempt to please the one loved. There is a willingness to sacrifice heart, mind, and soul for the one you love. We love God because He first loved us (1 John 4:19).

God, speaking in the first person, responds to the psalmist, "Because he has loved Me, I will deliver him." This means God will protect, rescue, and be with him in times of peril and trouble, protecting him from harm as revealed in verses one and four as he abides in the *shade* under the wings of the Almighty. It is a sense of "honor" that God bestows upon the one who loves Him.

*On high* is a haven, as in verse nine, which is a place that God puts the one who loves Him. It is a place where God dwells and is out of the reach of the "evils" pursuing him.

*Known my name*: The Hebrew word *yada* means "to know"—an intimacy, a closeness to God, having a longing for, or devotion to God.

In Exodus 3:13–15, Moses asked God, "What is your name?"

God stated, "*Ehyeh Asher Ehyeh*—I am who I am—I am the being. . .The LORD *(YHVH)*. . .this is My name forever, and thus I am to be remembered throughout all generations."

God names himself as the God who is, who was, and will be. In disclosing His name, God is revealing His mercy to His people.

*Ehyeh* (I Am) can also be translated "I will be what I will be." Simply, yet profoundly, God is always totally "I Am" or "I am the One who is." This is His name forever, and this is His title for all generations. God is saying you may call me by my name, but don't ever think you can fully comprehend me. "I am that I am. I exist; I will be who I will be."

God is God. He does not need us to confirm He exists—He profoundly "IS." He created us and then included us, offering us His Name. He reveals Himself to us. He lets

Himself be known. "I have manifested Your name to the men whom You gave Me out of the world; they were Yours and You gave them to Me, and they have kept Your word. . . . I have made Your name known to them, and will make it known, so that the love with which You loved Me may be in them, and I in them" (John 17:6, 26).

## POINTS TO PONDER

1. The one who loves God will be protected from harm as he abides in God's shade under His wings.
2. The one who loves God knows His name, implying intimacy and an abandonment of will, like a slave. Paul said he was a slave to Christ in which every part of his being belongs to God (Rom. 1:1; 2 Cor. 10:5).

May God bless us as we abide in God's shade, protected under His wings! Encourage one another during challenging times. Pray for one another, and bless your family and neighbor. We are "salt and light" in a world full of fear. Give them hope. The Gospel is hope.

## PRAYER

> Lord Jesus Christ, Keeper and Preserver of all things, let Thy right hand guard us by day and by night, when we sit at home, and when we walk abroad, when we lie down and when we rise up, that we may be kept from all evil, and have mercy upon us sinners. Amen.
>
> — Nerses of Clajes (AD 335–373)

PART NINE

# Behold, His Yeshua!

## Psalm 91:15–16

*"He will call upon Me, and I will answer him; I will be with him in trouble; I will rescue him and honor him. With a long life, I will satisfy him and let him see My salvation" (vv.15–16).*

*I WILL ANSWER HIM*: Religious Jews pray three times a day—morning, afternoon, and evening. These times were model by the Patriarchs: Abraham prayed in the morning, Genesis 19:27; Isaac prayed in the afternoon, Genesis 24:63; Jacob prayed at night, Genesis 32:9–22. God heard the psalmist prayers and answered Him.

*I will be with him in trouble; I will rescue him*: God is reassuring him that he will be protected from the enemy of physical or spiritual harm. God is reminding the psalmist that He will hold his hand and that He will help, saying "Do not fear" and I got you! (Isa. 41:13; cf. John 14:27)

*And honor him*: God will take away his troubles, and his neighbors will honor him as he was victorious over his enemies. His status in the community has now changed as he acknowledges it was God who brought the victory.

*Long life*: Psalm 90:10 reminds us of the shortness of life. However, sometimes, God gives us a long life with favor and satisfaction.

*Satisfy* comes from the Hebrew root *saba* or *sava* which means to be satisfied fully, continually. It is also the word used for grandfather—*saba*. A long life often brings the blessing of children and children's children. A grandparent is satisfied fully, indeed.

*See My salvation*: Our word "salvation" is *Yeshua* in the Hebrew. *Yeshua* is the Hebrew word for Jesus. Those who love God will see His *Yeshua*. Jesus said, "He who has seen Me has seen the Father" (John 14:9). Those who love God will behold Jesus. To love God is to love Jesus, for Jesus is God (John 1:1, 14).

## POINTS TO PONDER

1. Why do Jews pray 3 times a day?
    a. Blessings come when the sun rises; therefore, we praise Him (Lam. 3:22–24; Ps. 90:14).
    b. In the afternoon, as the sun begins to go down, we become concerned, we worry, and we begin to fear, so we pray (Ps. 94:19; 118:6).
    c. At night, in the complete darkness, danger lurks, and we cry out to God (Ps. 34:17–19).
2. Our days are numbered (Ps. 90:10, 12). Whether we have a long life or a short life, for those who love God, our eyes behold His *Yeshua* (Jesus, Salvation);

therefore, day by day and moment by moment, in the blessings and during trials, we will see Jesus!

May our eyes be full of Jesus during days of testing!

## PRAYER

In the evening and morning and noonday we praise Thee, we thank Thee, and pray Thee, Master of all, to direct our prayers as incense before Thee. Let not our hearts turn away to words or thoughts of wickedness, but keep us from all things that might hurt us; for to Thee, O Lord, our eyes look up, and our hope is in Thee: confound us not, O our God; for the sake of Jesus Christ our Lord. Amen.

—Eastern Church Vespers

Our Father and our God, we pray that in this period of crisis in our world that the Holy Spirit *will use it to remind us of our need of Thee and our relationship with Thee and we pray that tonight if our relationship is not right that we'll make it right through Jesus Christ our Lord who came to die on the cross because He loved us. For we ask it in His Name. Amen.*

—Billy Graham (Sacramento, California 1983)

# Bibliography


Blech, Benjamin. *More Secrets of Hebrew Words: Holy Days and Happy Days*. Northvale, NJ: Aronson, 1993.

———. *The Secrets of Hebrew Words*. Northvale, NJ: Aronson, 1991.

Bentorah, Chaim. *Hebrew Word Study: Revealing the Heart of God*. New Kensington, PA: Whitaker House, 2016.

Berlin, Adele, Marc Zvi Brettler, and Michael Fishbane. *The Jewish Study Bible*. New York: Oxford University, 2004.

Brenton, Sir Lancelot C. L. *The Septuagint with Apocrypho: Greek and English*. Hendrickson, 1851 and 2009.

Chambers, Oswald. *My Utmost for His Highest*. Westwood, NJ: Barbour and Company, Inc., 1963.

*JPS Hebrew-English Tanakh*. Philadelphia: The Jewish Publication Society, 1999.

Just, Arthur A., Jr. *Ancient Christian Commentary on Scripture, New Testament*. Vol. 3, *Luke*. Downers Grove, IL: InterVarsity, 2003.

*New American Standard Bible: Updated Edition*. La Habra, CA: The Lockman Foundation, 1960, 1962, 1963, 1968, 1971, 1972, 1973, 1975, 1977, 1995, 1996.

Novak, Al. *Hebrew Honey*. Houston: Countryman, 1987.

Phillips, John. *Exploring Genesis*. Neptune, NJ: Loizeaux, 1992.

Robertson, A. T. *Word Pictures in the New Testament, Concise Edition*. Nashville: Holman Bible, 2000.

Rozenberg, Martin S., and Bernard M. Zlotowitz. *The Book of Psalms: A New Translation and Commentary*. Northvale, NJ: Aronson, Inc., 1999.

Stern, David H. *The Complete Jewish Study Bible: Insights for Jews & Christians*. Peabody, MA: Hendrickson, 2016.

Vine, W. E. *An Expository Dictionary of New Testament Words*. Chicago: Moody, 1952.

Walvoord, John F., and Roy B. Zuck. *The Bible Knowledge Commentary, New Testament*. Wheaton, IL: Victor, 1983.

———. *The Bible Knowledge Commentary, Old Testament*. Wheaton, IL: Victor, 1985.

Prayers and Quotes taken from:

https://billygraham.org/story/5-prayers-for-america-from-billy-and-franklin-graham/; https://www.faithandworship.com/early_Christian_prayers.htm; https://www.gutenberg.org/files/48247/48247-h/48247-h.htm#c3; https://ryanphunter.wordpress.com/2012/11/23/saint-anthony-the-great-on-guardian-angels/